ballast

ballast

Quenton Baker

Haymarket Books
Chicago, Illinois

Published in 2023 by
Haymarket Books
P.O. Box 180165
Chicago, IL 60618
773-583-7884
www.haymarketbooks.org
info@haymarketbooks.org

ISBN: 978-1-64259-902-2

Distributed to the trade in the US through Consortium Book Sales and
Distribution (www.cbsd.com) and internationally through Ingram Pub-
lisher Services International (www.ingramcontent.com).

This book was published with the generous support of Lannan
Foundation and Wallace Action Fund.

Special discounts are available for bulk purchases by organizations and in-
stitutions. Please email info@haymarketbooks.org for more information.

Cover design by Jamie Kerry.

Printed in Canada by union labor.

Library of Congress Cataloging-in-Publication data is available.

10 9 8 7 6 5 4 3 2 1

Contents

ballast

Note

The first 94 pages of poems are redactions of Senate Document 51 of the Second Session of the 27th United States Congress in 1842. The document contains letters back and forth from the United States and British consulates in the Bahamas and sworn depositions from the white crew aboard the *Creole*. It was on that ship, in 1841, that 135 American-born enslaved people revolted and were able to escape chattel slavery. It is the only large-scale revolt of American-born enslaved peoples that did not end in capture, torture, or capital punishment. There is no known recorded speech or testimony from any of those 135 people.

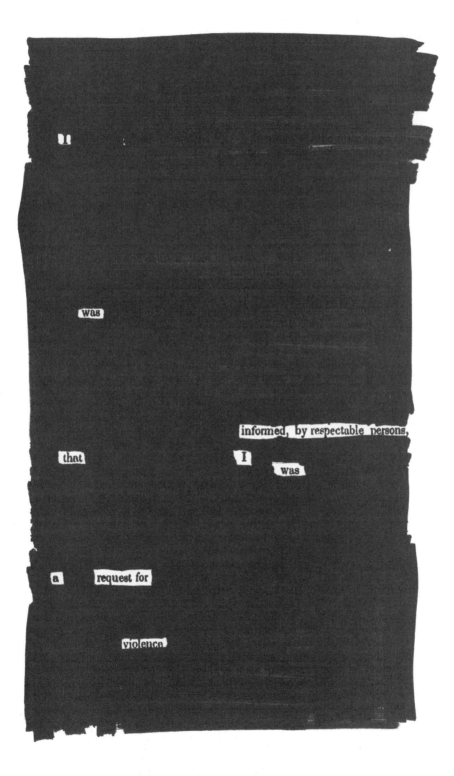

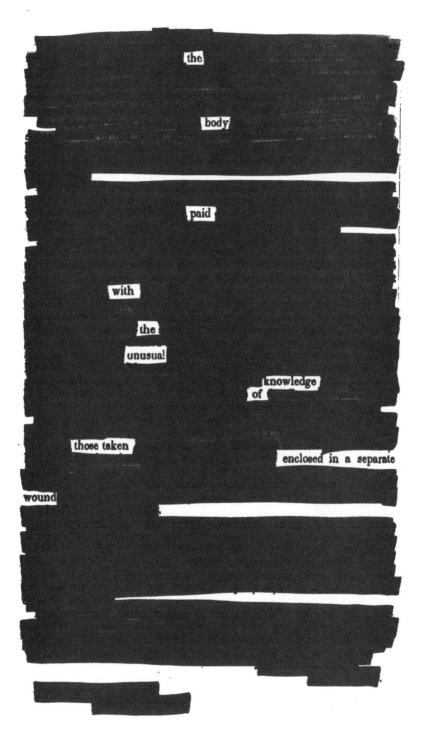

the

body

paid

with

the
unusual

knowledge
of

those taken

enclosed in a separate

wound

I have the honor

to

be

a portion of the cargo

lost to the owners.

I

am

several boats filled   black

I

am

several boats filled with   longing

I

had been the

urge

and

I

delivered the wished copies

thought proper

on arrival

returned

as

absence

make no resistance or blood would be spilt

paraded

if they pleased.

which being refused

the
necessary

wound

the

cost   in

testimony

I

was
a lantern in his hand

down and receive your message.

come

the

corpse

truck the light, and discovered

List of ██████████ *leaders* █████████ *Nassau, November 12,*
on board the brig Creole, ██████████████ 1841.

Madison Washington, Ben. Johnstone, or Blacksmith, Elijah Morris, Doctor Ruffin, George Grandy ████████████████████████████ Richard Butler, Phil. Jones, Robert Lumpkins, or Lumpley, Peter Smallwood, Harner Smith, Walter Brown, Adam Carney ██████, Horace Beverly, America, Addison Tyler, Wm. Jenkins, Pompey Garrison, George Basden, George Portlock—19.

confined

to be
persuaded

in language they could understand.

I am going up

God

of

the

knife

edge

body of

missed fire

of
blood to the handles

made

and

much bruised

fastened

to

a

fall.

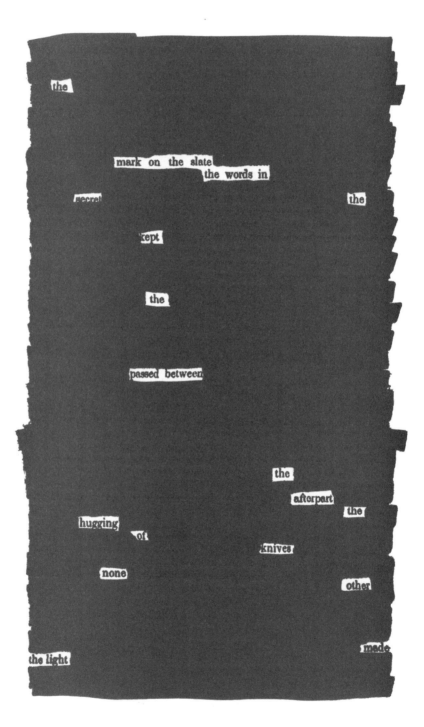

My

shout

and

passing

shore

concealed themselves on board

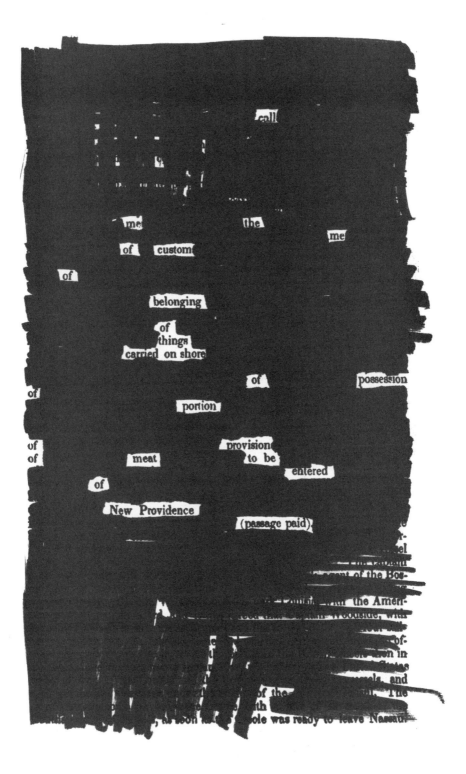

call

me the me

of custom

of

belonging

of
things
carried on shore

of possession

of

portion

of
of

meat provision
to be

entered

of

New Providence

(passage paid)

our

blood

at

a

convenient distance

the

night

called

out

in

color

every break in us   is   a treatise
on the perfect   fragile design of being
kept   the sail/tobacco leaf/night language
of waves/tongues as parcel

                  bless the island   bless the dim hum of un-slave
                bless each blade we buried in a deserving belly
                     we are cargo-born   ballast
                heavy with asking

                        and then what?

this ship   this pit for touch

this hospice   this thief of
the haptic

this maroonage   this slaughterhouse for bloom

this eerie lurch toward pillory and ash

curse

the bones of it

the open question   of our flesh

is the echo that orders the ocean

the sonorous snap   of the mast

we break   in ways that
please

of flesh as algorithm
of love as cipher

                    at that brutal crossing
                    we spoil what's linear
                    unwind chronology
                    spill the silken oil that demands us grist

we make our music from steady slip   or elision
foot slap in a black swamp
paint crash against vaulted fence
a bag full of language and style

                    there can be no end to us
                    we are not kinfolk with time
                    our clocks read nightmare and relief
                    are bright/variegated things
                    hands that reach toward redress
                    release

a breach
is night sound   possible

the potentiality of lurch
               lunch   for the cannonade

who need round gun
who need iron
                 the whole world is musket
                 all breath is a bullet   come home

and yet   we sip
     yet   we gasp
        yet   we kiss around the bang

                      we tear and are torn
                      in ragged enormity

negroes exist   *for the throwing*

every measure   percussive

every piece   a reason
                         to squeeze   to cut
                         to take

this knife
into   drum

this skin:

detonation

                         and then what?

ballast

on this ship   what can be named whole

we sleep   on a fixed pattern of chipped stone
we sleep   bricked in   with our beginnings

we sleep   in the finished sun
we sleep   through ruined moon
we sleep   in uniform
                     sewn-in

we sleep   allergic to ether
we sleep   badly behaved
we sleep   allergic to home/frantic return
we sleep   in constant bloody arrival

we sleep
and sleep
we sleep

swallowing bloom

we are disintegrated black
immune to referent

sediment spread by repeat burials
a misunderstood continental drift

oceanic trench of record skip

we brutish notes
thugs of the omitted

we parent break into bop
conjugate the aphotic into a flawless pyre

because what is funereal to the dead
we spin multiple graves simultaneous
new vinyl
speech across the deep

an ill language
ill-suited to surface
mis-fit for any proper kind of sink

shoal with the breaking waves
emerge from a spray of clink echo
we rattle-ghosts
lithograph of dark-lit motion
we wear the history of shatter as ornate cloak

        ocean as tipped bottle of rot perfume
        ship as open lesion
        we are a season of smoke cornered into consent
        ordered to burn

                no longer

we gather on shore
emissaries of the abyssal zone
curators of every hadal trench

         a deep black kinetic
         nutrient exchange in absolute exiguity

the ocean bangs
on closed cliff doors

who knows the blood
how to make it stain/how not

who can tell which shape is shadow   which is spear

can we conclude
is there a click/a flash of the blade   a brisk hug

of handspike at the end

or is that stain
always the runny middle

who will   at least   kill us right
                                                 kiss us shut

in a finished way

black is   open for empire

      black is ghost-home/ghost-ridden
               is glitch at full speed
      black is rugged door hung on lying church
               is matter of sick record
      black is leather/that leather is purse around silver
      black is almanac for exit wound
      black is blood authentic
               black is *not new to a knower*
               is steed ridden to froth
      black is kicking open the jaws of ghosts
               to holler proof toward clipped night

that long scream/split and spilling in the middle
wave/water/ship
we build and swallow it all
wet nurse to daggers in swaddling cloth

and then what?

still
yet we anthem toward altar

under such ambulatory pressure
rhythm should be rendered impossible

                    the whip burns in effigy of wound
                    lanterns at our hip
                              our steps warn the dusk

our nightmares fragment   into law
redolent phylactery of shell and discard
the world attuned to the fragrance
of overfed levee as statute
          of preteen   warded to the current

                    hull anthology
                    shattered through our entanglement
                    under red moon/chaste lightning

we de-legislate latitude
envelop border   in   kink and curve
collapse the lungs to unlatch the hold
our breath   bends   all barracoon skyward

look how far we come

                              what adroit steps we set as rigging
what litany   blade and bullet we pull tight for sail
what breach
we bloom bottle against

                 name   hull/guide   toward longer breath

blood don't run toward freedom/it just run
littoral/liturgical/a world-making emulsion

mixture of bone and spirit
unguent for civil society

how many touch thumb to forehead
in worship of distance   from this watched flesh

                         shadow in relief
                         a sharp wave made canonical through its breaking

and then what?

we are prayer in the long boat

> a rhizomatic scream
> surrounded by the dark dagger
> of the ocean

> scripture
> in its entirety
> anticipation of the lilt
> and yet

there is no word
for the rhythm
    we endure
    across this dirtless moment

> *antibird we sing like birds*
> textured and untrained

    rugged the love that claps
in the chasm of our black palms

and then what?

our rugged hands   irradiated with callus
emit navigatory black

                    become touchstone
                    a purity test for what's precious

               bent roughly   into bona fides

and we
        pulmonary sheathes
        for these praised
        bloodied utensils

                                we
                         grip wheel
                         clatter this ship
                         sick with manichean nightmares
                         toward shore

broken from out the middle
        combined
        our mouths be the o
            in cog

               love in us
                 mechanized
                   bruise
                   then blemish

             kept and bled
             supremacy
                 black

and then
             blacker still

blood of a long-curdled intimacy

breath calls out
        blade to scabbard
and our mouths
scan as militia

        and then what?

        we the lived-in rupture
        the recollection of breach

        a deeper love than any deity could imagine

        trench enough to bury the god of capital

a formal breach
deep within other breaking

        nesting doll of choke and control
        cavalcade of abandoning breath

lung as uninhabited peninsula
the promise of a road   commerce of breath

        enough to turn a spine liquid

to pour ourselves out

        toward a certain ending

that perpetual flay

grammar of the field
that writes us thrall

grammar of the ship
that turns wake to bowie

        knife edge slung along the underside of memory

we can cut chains
yet find no give
in the obsidian organs of the breach

that panoptic enormity
many-limbed and greedily liminal

our escape
a hinterland cartography
which turns every touch and release
a fresh refusal of the hold

slave

             as holy text
             as fiction of unlanguage
             as grotesque quartering

ordered via stigma

             we are
             performance and its end note
             coagulation and the necessary thinning

          we are
          everything worth looking for
          everything done to squeeze buck from bone
     a root/a rhizome
variegated/pursuing

                  in no need of discovery

for we are unto each other a shore

             every breaking wave an animating theft
             unlatched braid of heat and frost

to be a body

                              tied to season

is to be
a glitched wilderness

                    bent catalog of escape

to be
out from an outerself

                              in the burrow

                              in the tunnel

between tunnels

                                        we sit

a mosaic of self-theft

                              ear to walls of wood and dirt

                    to hear the secret language of cold salt
                    to echo louder than our cost
pressed   in calm cursive

we scrape within
grammar

for a price

bent bodies
form languid/illegible calligraphy

we write the field open
while buried beneath it

while harried inside it
banging on monied stalk
florid

fragrant

sack of labor

we write the ocean over
end of wave
end of rotten hull

the last thing
salt sees

ballast
big with sinew
lithe and gone

and so we shall continue
the perfection of discard

> golem empty of speech
> gilded by a filigreed absence

made to welcome any sudden fill

to wear exchange as a shining gown of silver wave
to know pleasure as unsigned promissory note

> its brief float in the foam of offshore breaking

we play thief to our own silhouette language
hidden within midnight's unctuous gristle

> two hands clasped
> the most mellifluous shovel
> to dig is beauty-in-circumstance
> provide a name to drape over the chasmic wound

in that shroud
we can forget
we must forgive the blood
before it spills

this ship is ritual improvisation
worship built around skull shape and improvement

        rough hewn bone
        girding a beguiled world perfect in its narrowing

        we are drained to a permanent acre of open thorn
        dense thicket of access and accumulation

we live through so much dark and distance
even the chronic collapse of nightmare is portal for origin

        model of the wound economy
        we pull ourselves closed
        chest flowering the most furious asylum

nation of rib/spinal connectivity
languishing in a retrograde slap of waves

emerging adorned in surf
enough   even if only for ourselves

and then what?

> biometric terror of release
> an opening up to like hands

> in a boundless era of adrenal misfire
> kin gathered within panorama of noose

> our love is forward-looking calisthenics
> thoracic ethos

jagged enough to decrypt the wave at its crest
jagged enough to unhitch the ocean from its gangrenous wagon
> to loosen one impossible hull
> with our impossible breath

brave to tunnel overboard
dig directly into ocean   body as spade

brave to stay in the hold's caliginous jaw
stomach-vectored flesh
swallowed to map the dimensions of the throat

> every back hoarded by wave is archival

ballast

every limb we press to shore is athenaeum in shadow

the breach met and endured
shaped with an unknowable lathe

imagine lending this much to the earth

and then what?

this ship deranges the sea

every break and swell is rupture in mosaic
every step in anticipation of ordinance
a black-on-black collage of refusal

we cry out to salt

home in the non-place of non-being

beseech black ligature of wave
to build us a new commons
move away from the dire selection of elective drowning

we do not rejoice in invasion preference
or re-brand of prison logic

we are black along a breach axis
property birthed enormous
uterine warehouse in a universe of escalation

bullet hold the lash for when it see us
chimerical warden of the borderlands
willing architect of an obliterating literature

we keep time within a flagellated firmament of skull
beloved bone woven into ancestral garments
both of and to protect from a lacerating chronology

in and from the waves
an infinite creative grammar

                                    we negate nation
                                    any king is a regrettable yet refuted echo
we unmake what makes us
metabolize entire singularity of rip current

neither super- nor sub-natural
yet unsculptable
arrayed through a certain breach
an ocean of rapid exit

                    and who hasn't been written open with a blade
                    air hot enough to cauterize the lungs
                    molestation so complete the skin forgets to peak and roll

pain stretched to fit/to fill
the world demands from us a habitable breaking

we refuse   via search   for a praxis that collapses the earth

from a terrigenous ontology
a ship full of continental theft and collapse

                    this catalyzing sea
                    the alchemical horror of the hold

built to transubstantiate a body to salt

        nightmare to law

                              chain to cuff

                    organ to flesh

            food to fence

dusk to flame
            flame to fingerprint

                        uterus to shed

and then what?

        we live

        burst from hulled chrysalis
        our names aerosoled as virus

        how wide and supple a back must be
        to rehome every bullet that finds us

        sick birth/grotesque conception

        humans transmuted to roachmule
        families diffused like corn flour

        we swallow black and come out black
        immunized/ a deified herd immunity

kiss in viral confinement
suck the venom from out soft/shining wave

we make the ocean ours
cartographical felons

        a fugitive blurring of border and stratum

entire planets in the offing
risen from out the seas we mark as navigational
to remake the world is light work

we love in an ocean of intrusion
we birth and rear within miasma of bullet

our most benign bops exude potentiality
andromeda falls out a two-step
we dap after long absence and zoom toward sunflower

come celebrate with us
on this steady bridge of knife and lash
we rejoice in our ordinary gait
our gifts given unto ourselves
what do we see except infinite inquiry

and then what?

all narrative is sick with our resonance
thundering murmur/cyclone of good whisper

we fly a seismic kite
      between barracoon bars
      between slats in the hull

                a deep/episodic message
                escaping in and from the blood

every wave emerges from our flesh gone quiet
the interlocking matrices of our hush

        we womb and wean abyss
        love it almost full/give it our name
        what some imagine as hell/we know as late evening

wrap landscape around last night's thigh
fold the horizon into gingham
for a train ride toward a parallel star

> we turn this ship into rail and spike
> rewrite mast into peanut oil
> fry the entire sun with cayenne and sage

another day will not set on this flayed arrangement
hunt the frame to obliterate the frame

we gut the masculine mistake of control and possession

> our knife is a map honed outside of time
> we make cuts that ignore duration
> score the earth in a pleasing pattern

we shatter where we step
each shard of broken bark recalls shadow
each shadow is voice in resin

> honeyed sap slipping toward speech
> a thick/invigorating condition
> to end this clay's horror sequence

and then what?

economy of cut and mark
palimpsestic flesh
closed up and scored again
to reenact color's arrival

        we barter in stigma narrative
        trade interior lash story for a dwindling snap
        weak dollars dangled into palsied mouths

        a side hustle panopticon
        reinvention in full view
        align our very breath to plummet the coin

we scar into propulsion
summon dirt as bitter shawl

        wear the earth to erase the world
        with a blade banged out during third shift

we curse the necrotic wave
a vile roil of limb and fetid crest

our touch
in this sharp-starred night
we ablute the shore

slaughter this dysgenic world

of solar throats slashed as stylistic hallmark
of black skin as ink pot for flourish

our flesh   the kaleidoscopic tilt of dollars toward death

its bare life   in a confluence of iron

our assembly   critiques the genre

an awareness-cum-refusal of the sickly hieroglyphic

semiotic purge through consensual body rock

new syllables shaped around spasmodic collapse

the internal apocalypse at climax

we are   a tear in this   hostile finish

the coffle   grottos the blood
thrum language pumped subterranean
flesh made lexical
                    de-housed from fieldstone

we demand the earth return us

            in the grammar of   bone-spitting oak
            in the grammar   of limb-chewing wave
            irrupt the firing pin
            collapse trigger until it resembles an unlit waning

      an   unhitched   wailing

                  we will not modulate or vary the tone
                  a suturing shout
                  in un-unison
                  broad stalactite of threat and futurity

the dirt   is a dialect

we drip   underneath

we lustral bloodbearers
perfecters of spill
          unkillable/fugitive dead

                    our eluted flesh
                    cleansed of every grope and clinch

our wrack-weighted cots
slashed and wrapped in asafetida

                    black market of redress
                    we donate one other to ourselves
                    the proceeds of survival

assemblage-in-wave
the elision of the hold

                    to occupy the badlands between break and escape
                    between breach and too much

                    yes   we will cut the head off a snake
                    build panorama from its end

treat any scrap of planet like juniper seed

Washing the Bones

> *"The intent of this practice is not to give voice to the slave, but rather to imagine what cannot be verified, a realm of experience which is situated between two zones of death—social and corporeal death— and to reckon with the precarious lives which are visible only in the moment of their disappearance. It is an impossible writing which attempts to say that which resists being said. . . . It is a history of an unrecoverable past; it is a narrative of what might have been or could have been; it is a history written with and against the archive."*
>
> **—Saidiya Hartman, "Venus in Two Acts"**

When I set out to work on this book, in the initial research phases, I had a completely different idea of where I was headed. When I read about the revolt aboard the brig *Creole*, the only successful, large-scale revolt of American-born enslaved people, I thought that I would uncover something, anything, about the 135 people (roughly, accounts vary) that were on the ship and build a work around their lives. But the more I looked, all I found was erasure; a re-writing or a dramatization at best, or a total disappearance at worst.

So I had to switch to a kind of excavation, or perhaps, retribution. Of the extant documents, and there weren't many, Senate document 51, from the 2nd session of the 27th Congress in 1842 felt like the logical choice: to return a facsimile of the rupture; something to drill down into and break apart into a different logic. This document is primarily made up of depositions from the white slavers on the *Creole* and correspondence between the United States and British consulates on Nassau. I think I would say I had no choice. Beyond the very limited material on this revolt to begin with, once I encountered the Senate document and read the kind of erasure and obliteration replicated in it, I don't think I had any other option except to use it as the text for this project.

Simply put, it made me angry, and I wanted to do something with that anger. Rage and anger and violence are byproducts of living in an anti-black world. There are only so many places that I can put it that won't get me killed or harm someone that I don't want to harm. But when I read this Senate document, I wanted to harm it. I wanted to visit a certain kind of violence upon it. And so I did.

I wanted to cause hurt. Not toward the reader but toward the text. A kind of habitable hurt, a violence you could live in. There are people in the document, but they exist as object. They are referred to by the white slavers or by the white diplomats. The leaders of the rebellion are sometimes mentioned by name. But there is nothing approaching an I, nothing internal, nothing in anyone's own tongue (of course even if it were present, it would be under duress).

I see the Senate document both as a text and urtext, in a sense. It is an original (and, of course, profoundly unoriginal) blueprint of the kind of obliteration that happened/happens to the slave. The slave does not exist; the slave is non-being; the slave occupies the object position of the socially dead. So a document like this Senate record, even if it did have the voice of the enslaved, couldn't actually contain them; they would always be buried beneath it, or rather they'd always be the negative space that made the text legible and coherent. So it was less about uncovering or excavating or speaking for or finding, because that would be impossible given the condition of the slave. It's unknowable. But I could listen for echoes, *imagine what could not be verified*, and that's how I think of these poems: as echoes, as ghosts, as penitent imaginings. The I's that appear are a kind of resonance or reverberation that sounds when you strike a blow, when you tear apart a text like this.

Another vital consideration for me throughout this process was audience and language. What does it mean when your only visibility to the archive (or to the world at large) is through your pained body, your death, your unjust and early end? What does it mean to live in-between all that? The monstrous reality of a perilous life, balanced against the normal/mundane/wonderful things that can happen in a human's day-to-day existence. Caught inside social death, or non-being, but of course you're fully alive to your loved ones, to your community. And it all matters. You can't elide or omit any of it, but neither can you pretend that a portion is the whole story either.

So my consideration of audience and language are tied to that double life. I want black folks to feel seen, understood, in all of that complexity that comes from life on the knife's edge. But it still is life. We've built it; we survive in it; we make the uninhabitable habitable. And I think that's the project that I try to attend to in this book. How to make this alien and terrible world that requires our death habitable. How to celebrate our survival in it without limiting us to only our survival. How to address trauma without reenacting it, or give life to the thinking that makes up the totality of who we are.

Of course, I don't decide who interacts with my work, but I think my consideration begins and ends with black folks. Because of the nature of the work, I don't think I can really imagine audience beyond that. Because my main considerations are harm (as in not doing it) and redress (offering it, however flawed it must be). If my goal is to avoid the fraught, dangerous semiotics of English in regards to blackness, and it is, then that takes all of my attention and whatever linguistic skill I might have. Working in this language, one that is so heavy with terrible hooks into and from the white imagination, which is thick with so much horrible history and harm, so much layered danger in terms of associations, I feel like I have to clean my words, wash my bones, before I can present them properly.

The other main focus for this project was time. It's both linear and not, temporal and atemporal simultaneously, similar to how blackness exists outside of time yet also structures chronology. The erasures are absolutely structured by whatever time existed on the *Creole* and are dealing with the echoes of those 135 people, but also those structures affect us still and bleed out beyond any attempt at chronology. The second section of the book exists in whatever time currently structures black life, which both is and is not the structure crushing those on the *Creole*. Nothing is clean or clearly delineated in this type of world-spanning non-being.

Part of my goal for the book was to collapse the distance between those two seemingly distinct periods of time, to lay one over the other like two tracings of the same horrible glyph. And that was an animating force for me. How to live in the midst of these colossal, terrifying, and yet ultimately insufficient acts of liberation and meaning-making. The atemporality comes from the fact that, of course, we still live in these survival choices. We can't escape a world that has codified black non-being, but we also can't fully live in it, because our humanity is conditional and obliteration looms.

For example, there were 135 enslaved people aboard that ship, and only eighteen were involved in the revolt. We don't/can't know how many of the 135 knew and declined to participate or if they just weren't made aware. We have no way to make an inventory of their decisions. But we do know that five people elected to stay on the ship and return to New Orleans. And perhaps more than the eighteen that took control of the ship, those five have stuck in my brain. It's impossible to understand decision making in the face of an obliterating horror as complete as chattel slavery. We'll never know why those five people chose to return to the United States, but it illuminated a larger point that I thought was really important to the project. It's easy for us to look at something like a slave revolt and think of it as a positive story, an end to captivity. An escape. But it's an escape taking place, still, within an anti-black world obsessed with capital, enabled by a different colonial power through absorption into a different colony.

So I wanted to occupy the interiority of those decisions, and the similar ones that black folks still make on a daily, hourly, moment-to-moment basis. Not to report on it, or to make it plain to a world that doesn't deserve to see it, but to simply acknowledge its (and our) existence. As a testament to us, to black life, black meaning-making as we live life under constraint.

Acknowledgements

Earlier versions of excerpts from this book have appeared in *jubilat*, *Poetry Northwest*, *the Offing*, *Small Po[r]tions*, *Splinter*, Poets.org Poem-a-Day, *the Rumpus*, *Pinwheel*, *the Volta*, and *the James Franco Review*. A portion of the redactions were also published as a chapbook with Paul Hlava Ceballos and appeared in an exhibition at the Frye Art Museum.

"negroes exist for the throwing" is from M. NourbeSe Philip's *Zong!*

"not new to a knower" is from Amiri Baraka's "The City of New Ark: A Poem of Destiny."

"unlatched braid of heat and frost" is from Gwendolyn Brooks' "Riders to the Blood-Red Wrath."

"antibird, we sing like birds" is from Nathaniel Mackey's *Nod House*.

Bibliography

Will Alexander, *Above the Human Nerve Domain* (Columbus: Pavement Saw Press, 1998).

Dionne Brand, *A Map to the Door of No Return: Notes to Belonging* (Toronto: Vintage Canada, 2003).

Gwendolyn Brooks, *Selected Poems* (New York: Harper Perennial, 2006).

———. *Report from Part One* (Detroit: Broadside Press, 1973).

Simone Browne, *Dark Matters: On the Surveillance of Blackness* (Durham: Duke University Press, 2015).

Aimé Césaire, *The Collected Poetry* (Berkeley and Los Angeles: University Of California Press, 1983).

———. *Discourse on Colonialism* (New York: Monthly Review Press, 2001).

St. Clair Drake, *Black Folk Here and There* (Brooklyn: Diasporic Africa Press, 2014).

Frederick Douglass, *The Heroic Slave: A Cultural and Critical Edition* (New Haven: Yale University Press, 2015).

Arthur T. Downey, *The Creole Affair: The Slave Rebellion that Led the U.S. and Great Britain to the Brink of War* (Lanham: Rowman & Littlefield, 2014).

Henry Dumas, *Knees of a Natural Man: The Selected Poetry of Henry Dumas* (New York: Thunder's Mouth Press, 1989).

Rachel Blau Duplessis, *Genders, Races, and Religious Cultures in Modern American Poetries, 1908-1934* (Cambridge: Cambridge University Press, 2001).

Frantz Fanon, *Black Skin, White Masks* (New York: Grove Press, 2008).

Denise Ferreira da Silva, *Toward a Global Idea of Race* (Minneapolis: University Of Minnesota Press, 2007).

Paul Gilroy, *The Black Atlantic: Modernity and Double Consciousness* (Brooklyn and London: Verso Books, 1993).

Édouard Glissant, *Poetics of Relation* (Ann Arbor: University Of Michigan Press, 1997).

Alexis Pauline Gumbs, *M Archive* (Durham: Duke University Press, 2018).

Saidiya Hartman, *Lose Your Mother* (New York: Farrar, Straus and Giroux, 2007).

———. *Scenes of Subjection* (Oxford: Oxford University Press, 1997).

———. "The Position of the Unthought," *Qui Parle,* vol. 13, no. 2, (2003): 183–201.

———. "Venus in Two Acts," *Small Axe* 26, vol. 12, no. 2 (2008): 1–14.

George Hendrick and Willene Hendrick, *The Creole Mutiny: A Tale of Revolt Aboard a Slave Ship* (Chicago: Ivan R. Dee, 2003).

Alan Jamieson, *The Hadal Zone: Life in the Deepest Oceans* (Cambridge: Cambridge University Press, 2015).

Tyehimba Jess, *Olio* (Seattle: Wave Books, 2016).

Walter Johnson, *Soul by Soul: Life inside the Antebellum Slave Market* (Cambridge: Harvard University Press, 2009).

———. *The Chattel Principle: Internal Slave Trades in the Americas* (New Haven: Yale University Press, 2004).

Nathaniel Mackey, *Nod House* (New York: New Directions, 2011).

Manning Marable, *How Capitalism Underdeveloped Black America: Problems in Race, Political Economy, and Society* (Chicago: Haymarket Books, 2015).

Dawn Lundy Martin, *Life in a Box Is a Pretty Life* (Brooklyn: Nightboat Books, 2015).

Katherine McKittrick, *Demonic Grounds: Black Women and the Cartographies of Struggle* (Minneapolis: University Of Minnesota Press, 2006).

———. *Sylvia Wynter: On Being Human as Praxis* (Durham: Duke University Press, 2015).

Edmund Morgan, *American Slavery, American Freedom* (New York: W.W. Norton, 1975).

Fred Moten, *Black and Blur* (Durham: Duke University Press, 2017).

———. *Hughson's Tavern* (Providence, RI: Leon Works, 2008).

———. *In the Break: The Aesthetics of the Black Radical Tradition* (Minneapolis: University of Minnesota Press, 2003).

———.*Stolen Life* (Durham: Duke University Press, 2018).

———. *The Service Porch* (Seattle: Letter Machine Editions, 2016).

Fred Moten and Stefano Harney, *A Poetics of the Undercommons* (Brooklyn: Sputnik & Fizzle, 2016).

Aldon Lynn Nielsen, *Black Chant: Languages of African-American Postmodernism* (Cambridge: Cambridge University Press, 1997).

———. *Integral Music: Languages of African American Innovation* (Tuscaloosa: University Of Alabama Press, 2004).

———. *Reading Race* (Athens: University of Georgia Press, 1988).

Aldon Lynn Nielsen and Lauri Ramey, *Every Goodbye Ain't Gone: An Anthology of Innovative Poetry by African Americans* (Tuscaloosa: University Of Alabama Press, 2006).

M. NourbeSe Philip, *Blank: Essays & Interviews* (Toronto: Book*hug, 2017).

———. *She Tries Her Tongue, Her Silence Softly Breaks* (Middletown: Wesleyan University Press, 2015).

———. *Zong!* (Middletown: Wesleyan University Press, 2008).

Carlo Rovelli, *The Order of Time* (London: Allen Lane, 2018).

Patricia Saunders, "Fugitive Dreams of Diaspora: Conversations with Saidiya Hartman." *Anthurium: A Caribbean Studies Journal*, vol. 6, no. 1 (2008): 7.

Christina Sharpe, *In the Wake: On Blackness and Being* (Durham: Duke University Press, 2016).

———. *Monstrous Intimacies: Making Post-Slavery Subjects* (Durham: Duke University Press, 2010).

C. Riley Snorton, *Black on Both Sides: A Racial History of Trans Identity* (Minneapolis: University Of Minnesota Press, 2017).

Jack Spicer, *My Vocabulary Did This to Me: The Collected Poetry of Jack Spicer* (Middletown: Wesleyan University Press, 2010).

Hortense J. Spillers, *Black, White, and in Color: Essays on American Literature and Culture* (Chicago: University Of Chicago Press, 2003).

———. "Mama's Baby, Papa's Maybe: An American Grammar Book," *Diacritics*, vol. 17, no. 2 (1987): 64–81.

Lorenzo Thomas, *Extraordinary Measures* (Tuscaloosa: University of Alabama Press, 2000).

Frank B. Wilderson III, *Incognegro* (Durham: Duke University Press, 2015).

———. *Red, White & Black* (Durham: Duke University Press, 2010).

Calvin L. Warren, *Ontological Terror: Blackness, Nihilism, and Emancipation* (Durham and London: Duke University Press, 2018).

Alexander G. Weheliye, *Habeas Viscus: Racializing Assemblages, Biopolitics, and Black Feminist Theories of the Human* (Durham: Duke University Press, 2014).

Michelle M. Wright, *Physics of Blackness* (Minneapolis: University of Minnesota Press, 2015).

Sylvia Wynter, "Unsettling the Coloniality of Being/Power/Truth/Freedom: Towards the Human, after Man, Its Overrepresentation—an Argument," *CR: The New Centennial Review*, vol. 3, no. 3 (2003): 257–337.

About the Author

Quenton Baker is a poet, educator, and Cave Canem fellow. Their current focus is black interiority and the afterlife of slavery. Their work has appeared in *The Offing*, *jubilat*, *Vinyl*, *The Rumpus*, and elsewhere. They are a two-time Pushcart Prize nominee and the recipient of the 2018 Arts Innovator Award from Artist Trust. They were a 2019 Robert Rauschenberg Artist in Residence and a 2021 NEA Fellow. They are the author of *This Glittering Republic* (Willow Books, 2016) and *we pilot the blood* (The 3rd Thing, 2021)

About Haymarket Books

Haymarket Books is a radical, independent, nonprofit book publisher based in Chicago. Our mission is to publish books that contribute to struggles for social and economic justice. We strive to make our books a vibrant and organic part of social movements and the education and development of a critical, engaged, and internationalist Left.

We take inspiration and courage from our namesakes, the Haymarket Martyrs, who gave their lives fighting for a better world. Their 1886 struggle for the eight-hour day—which gave us May Day, the international workers' holiday—reminds workers around the world that ordinary people can organize and struggle for their own liberation. These struggles—against oppression, exploitation, environmental devastation, and war—continue today across the globe.

Since our founding in 2001, Haymarket has published more than nine hundred titles. Radically independent, we seek to drive a wedge into the risk-averse world of corporate book publishing. Our authors include Angela Y. Davis, Arundhati Roy, Keeanga-Yamahtta Taylor, Eve L. Ewing, Aja Monet, Mariame Kaba, Naomi Klein, Rebecca Solnit, Olúfẹ́mi O. Táíwò, Mohammed El-Kurd, José Olivarez, Noam Chomsky, Winona LaDuke, Robyn Maynard, Leanne Betasamosake Simpson, Howard Zinn, Mike Davis, Marc Lamont Hill, Dave Zirin, Astra Taylor, and Amy Goodman, among many other leading writers of our time. We are also the trade publishers of the acclaimed Historical Materialism Book Series.

Haymarket also manages a vibrant community organizing and event space in Chicago, Haymarket House, the popular Haymarket Books Live event series and podcast, and the annual Socialism Conference.